Contents

Wayne Rooney

ENGLISH HITMAN

Rooney is an energetic player on the pitch. He runs around 12km each game!

Stats!

Name: Wayne Mark Rooney

Date of birth: 24 October 1985

Clubs: Everton (2002-04), Manchester United (2004-present)

Position: Striker

First break: Rooney joined Everton as a schoolboy, and rose through the ranks. Five days before his 17th birthday, he made his professional debut against Arsenal. He scored the winning goal, ending Arsenal's 30-match unbeaten run, and became the youngest goal scorer in Premier League history.

Major achievements: With Manchester United Rooney has won the Premier League three times (2006-07, 2007-08 and 2008-09) and the Champions League in 2008. He has also won the PFA Young Player of the Year award twice (2004-05 and 2005-06) and the PFA and Football Writers' Player of the Year awards in 2009-10. In 2012 he scored two goals in his 500th senior career game.

Secrets of success: Rooney is one of the country's most naturally gifted players, and a great goal scorer. He is also a hard worker, who always gives 100 per cent.

Rooney played for Everton Under-9s against Manchester United and scored six goals, including a perfect overhead kick!

Life Story

Wayne Rooney burst onto the Premiership scene as a 16 year old in 2002 with a wonder goal against Arsenal, and has not looked back since. After two years with his hometown club Everton, he became Britain's most expensive teenager when he joined Manchester United in August 2004 for £25.6 million. Since then he has won just about every trophy in the English game.

As the first choice striker for his team and for England, Rooney has to shoulder the burden or responsibility for his team's success. At times, including the 2010 World Cup in South Africa, it can be a lot to handle, but mostly he rises to the challenge and plays with the infectious energy and enthusiasm of a schoolboy; chasing around the pitch and challenging for every ball.

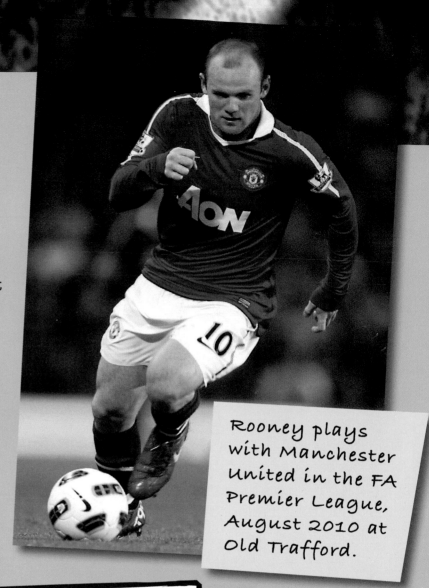

Rooney plays with Manchester United in the FA Premier League, August 2010 at Old Trafford.

Questions and Answers

Q **You seem to work very hard on the pitch, helping your defenders as well as trying to score goals?**

A "You know, I do that because I want to win. I should probably save my energy and stay up front, but I think it's just the way I have been brought up. I want to win and I try to give everything to do that."

Wayne Rooney, the *Mirror*, February 2010

Q **As a striker, you often get the credit when your team wins. Is that fair?**

A "No. Football is a team game and it's the whole team that should take credit, not just individual players. Every member of the squad plays their part and as a team we win together and we lose together."

Wayne Rooney, fourfourtwo.com, 2009

When his strike partner Cristiano Ronaldo left Manchester United for Real Madrid, fans were worried they would miss Ronaldo's goals. Instead, Rooney stepped into Cristiano Ronaldo's shoes and enjoyed his greatest goal scoring season with 34 goals, 26 in the Premier League. Rooney never ever wants to be beaten!

Cristiano Ronaldo

THE £80 MILLION MAN

Ronaldo celebrates after scoring in the World Cup in Cape Town in 2010.

At Manchester United, Ronaldo stayed behind at training for 30 minutes every day just practising free kicks.

Stats!

Name: Cristiano Ronaldo dos Santos Aveiro

Date of birth: 5 February 1985

Clubs: Sporting Lisbon in Portugal (2001-03), Manchester United (2003-09), Real Madrid in Spain (2009-present)

Position: Winger

First break: Ronaldo joined his local team Andorinha when he was eight. Two years later he signed with CD Nacional and, after helping them win the youth league, he was offered a trial with Sporting Lisbon. He joined Lisbon's academy and was the only player to play for Under-16s, Under-17s, Under-18s, the B-team and the first team all in the same season!

Major achievements: Won the Premier League three times with Manchester United (2006-07, 2007-08, 2008-09), the FA Cup (2004) and the Champions League (2008). He was named European Player of the Year in 2007, and World Player of the Year in 2008.

Secrets of success: Ronaldo is a master of the dribble – fast, with great close ball control. His free kicks are also legendary. According to experts, he is able to generate speed and dip on the ball by shifting his bodyweight forward and 'slicing' his foot across the ball on impact.

Life Story

When Ronaldo moved to Manchester as an 18 year old from his home in Madeira, Portugal, he was so homesick he used to cry every time he spoke to his family on the telephone. Now the world's most expensive footballer – who joined Real Madrid for a massive £80 million in the summer of 2009 – remembers those times as helping him develop the necessary mental toughness to succeed in his chosen profession.

Questions and Answers

Q When did you start playing football?

A "I started to play in Madeira in the street. The kids there still love to play football... From an early age my dream was to become a professional footballer, I did it and now I can say: never give up. Opportunities come to [everyone], we must know how to grasp them."

Cristiano Ronaldo, the *Mirror*, January 2009

Q You're fast, you can dribble and you score great goals. What makes you special?

A "I was born this way! But if you have quality and do not train every day you will go nowhere."

Cristiano Ronaldo, realmadridzone.com, 2010

During Ronaldo's six years in Manchester, he grew from a talented, but often frustrating player into a guaranteed match winner. In the 2007-08 season, he broke George Best's 40-year record for the most goals scored by a midfield player – 42 in all competitions. Season after season he grew quicker, stronger, his free kicks more accurate, and he became so important to the team, that Manchester United fans worried about how their team would cope without him!

In Spain, Ronaldo has continued his goal scoring form, with 26 goals in his first season. Madrid were beaten to the title by an amazing Barcelona team, but no one would bet against Ronaldo helping Real lift the Spanish title very soon.

Ronaldo plays for Portugal against the Czech Republic in Geneva in 2008.

Steven Gerrard

LIVERPOOL'S SUPERMAN

The IGOAL campaigners, including Gerrard, meet at Downing Street in March 2010.

Stats!

Name: Steven George Gerrard

Date of birth: 30 May 1980

Clubs: Liverpool (1998–present)

Position: Centre midfield

First break: Gerrard was spotted by Liverpool scouts at eight years old playing for his hometown team Whiston Juniors. He joined Liverpool's youth academy at nine, and signed his first professional contract in November 1997. Gerrard made his first team debut in November 1998, and played 13 times that season, often as a replacement for the team's injured captain Jamie Redknapp.

Major achievements: Gerrard won the Champions League with Liverpool in 2005. He has also won two FA Cups (2001, 2006), two League Cups (2001, 2003), and a UEFA Cup (2001). In 2009, he was named Footballer Writers' Player of the Year.

Secrets of success: Steven Gerrard has all the skills a modern footballer needs. He is fast, a great tackler, can pass the ball long or short, and can score not only spectacular but also important goals. His goals in the 2005 Champions League and 2006 FA Cup Finals took both games into extra time, and helped Liverpool win the trophies.

Steven Gerrard's inspiration is his cousin Jon-Paul, who died in the 1989 Hillsborough tragedy that killed 96 football fans.

Life Story

Steven Gerrard is the ultimate competitor. As someone who was born in Liverpool, and has played for one club his entire career, he is his team's main source of inspiration. He leads by example and never stops trying to bring success to Liverpool. He was named Man of the Match in Liverpool's Champions League final victory in 2005, and the FA Cup Final win the following year.

Gerrard made his England debut in 2000. He played in the 2000 and 2004 European Championships, and the 2006 and 2010 World Cups. In South Africa, he was made England captain when Rio Ferdinand's knee injury forced him to miss the tournament. Gerrard was one of the team's most consistent performers, and scored in the 1-1 draw with the USA.

Steven scores the opening goal against the USA in the World Cup in June 2010.

Questions and Answers

Q What's it like playing under a foreign manager?

A "I've worked with plenty of foreign coaches and it's been brilliant. Gerard Houllier and Rafa Benitez [for Liverpool], and [Sven-Goran] Eriksson and [Fabio] Capello for England. These are football people, they're winners. It doesn't matter what nationality they are... It's brought me on as a player and I feel like I've learned from their contrasting methods."

Steven Gerrard, fourfourtwo.com, 2008

Q What would it feel like to win the Premier League with Liverpool?

A "To win the title here, at Liverpool, would mean a lot more than winning seven or eight trophies at another club. Here, I can share it with my family, with the Liverpool supporters. I have always been one of them."

Steven Gerrard, the *Mirror*, June 2009

Gerrard has won several awards. He was named PFA Young Player of the Year in 2000 and PFA Player of the Year in 2006, and has been included in the PFA Team of the Year for the past six seasons. In 2007 he received an MBE (Master of the British Empire) from the Queen.

David Villa

SPANISH HITMAN

Barcelona's new signing, David Villa, at Camp Nou Stadium in May 2010 in Barcelona.

Stats!

Name: David Villa Sánchez

Date of birth: 3 December 1981 in Tuilla, Asturias, Spain

Clubs: Sporting Gijón (1999-03), Real Zaragoza (2003-05), Valencia (2005-10), Barcelona (2010-present)

Position: Striker

First break: Villa grew up in the northern Spanish region of Asturias. He had trials for one of the area's biggest teams, Real Oviedo, but was turned down because he was too short (he is only 5ft 9in today). Luckily, he was accepted at another local club, Sporting Gijón. He worked his way through the youth ranks, and made his first team debut in 2000.

Major achievements: Villa won the Copa del Rey (the equivalent of the FA Cup) with Real Zaragoza in 2004 and with Valencia in 2008. Most importantly, he is Spain's all-time top scorer and has helped his country win Euro 2008 and the 2010 World Cup.

Secrets of success: Villa is naturally right-footed, but broke his right leg when he was a child. While his leg was in plaster, his father threw a football to him for hours, forcing him to kick with his left foot. He is now just as deadly with both feet!

Villa has his daughter Zaida's name embroidered on one football boot, and the Spanish flag on the other.

Life Story

David Villa is one of the world's best strikers. Until his move to Barcelona in summer 2010 for £32 million, he had never played for one of Europe's biggest clubs, but his excellent ball control, clever movement, and deadly shooting accuracy have seen him score nearly 200 goals for some of Spain's smaller teams.

Questions and Answers

Q Who has been the biggest influence on your career?

A "My dad has always supported me, and cheered me up until my career came around. I can barely remember a single training session when [he] wasn't there. I have never been alone on a football pitch."

David Villa, soccerlens.com, 2008

Q Who is your perfect strike partner?

A "Fernando Torres. We complement each other very well. We get on well on the pitch and very well off it too. We're a good partnership. We chase down defenders, put pressure on and fight to create chances for each other. We work well together."

David Villa, the *Scotsman*, June 2009

Villa began his career in the Spanish Second Division, scoring an average of one goal every two games for Sporting Gijón. He kept up the average when he transferred to Real Zaragoza in the First Division, and then scored 101 goals in just 180 appearances for his former club Valencia.

He has enjoyed most success with the Spanish national team. Spain ended a 44-year wait for an international trophy by winning Euro 2008, and although Villa missed the final through injury, he scored four goals in the four games he played, making him the tournament's top scorer. He is also Spain's top scorer in World Cup finals, with eight goals (three in 2006, and five in 2010). Defenders, beware of the Spanish hitman!

Villa in a Spanish League match between RCD Espagnol and Valencia in May 2010.

Carlos Tévez

BACKSTREET HERO

Tévez is revealed as the new Manchester City signing in July 2009.

When Tévez played for Corinthians, he was the first non-Brazilian to win their Player of the Year award in 30 years!

Stats!

Name: Carlos Alberto Tévez (born Carlos Alberto Martínez)

Date of birth: 5 February 1984

Clubs: Boca Juniors in Argentina (2001-04), Corinthians in Brazil (2004-06), West Ham United (2006-07), Manchester United (2007-09), Manchester City (2009-present)

Position: Striker

First break: Tévez was spotted playing football in the street, and signed by his first club, All Boys, at just eight years old. At 13 he joined Boca Juniors' youth team, scoring 70 goals in four years.

Major achievements: He won the league with Boca Juniors (2002-03) and Corinthians (2004-05), and the Premier League (2007-08, 2008-09) and Champions League (2008) with Manchester United. He also won a Gold medal with Argentina at the 2004 Olympics. He was given two Player of the Year awards in 2010, and also made club captain until 2011.

Secrets of success: Tévez grew up in one of the most dangerous neighbourhoods in Buenos Aires, known for its violence, drugs and poverty. His father was often out of work, and his mother stayed at home to bring up Tévez and his four brothers and sisters. He developed his football skills playing street football in return for money to feed his family.

Life Story

Carlos Tévez grew up in the slums of Ejército de los Andes, playing football on the streets to earn money to buy food and drink. A born fighter, he brings the same determination and will to win to all the professional teams he has represented.

At 10 months old Tévez poured a kettle of boiling water over himself, causing third degree burns and putting him in hospital for two months. The accident left him with a scar on the right side of his face, neck and chest. However, he refused to have plastic surgery as a series of operations would have stopped him playing football for four months! He later refused an offer from his first professional team Boca Juniors to have the scars cosmetically improved, saying they were a part of 'who he was in the past and who he is today'.

Tévez with Manchester City play against Liverpool in the FA Premier League, 2010.

Tévez is a fierce competitor with an excellent scoring record. His goals saved West Ham United from relegation in 2007, and he found the net 23 times in 35 appearances in his first season at Manchester City. Tévez plays to win.

Questions and Answers

Q **Who are the best fans you have played in front of?**

A "West Ham. Their supporters 'feel' football. They are passionate. These people invested great support in me. I want to play for West Ham again before I finish my career. I have some unfinished business there."

Q **Which sportsmen do you most admire?**

A "Tiger Woods, Roger Federer and Lionel Messi. They perform with excellence, like most of us could never dream of... These men create history with their level of performances. It is sport at another level. They are winning machines."

Carlos Tévez, the *Daily Mail*, April 2010 (both quotes)

Wesley Sneijder

DEAD BALL SPECIALIST

Sneijder lifts the UEFA Champions League trophy after the final against Bayern Munich, 2010.

Stats!

Name: Wesley Benjamin Sneijder

Date of birth: 9 June 1984

Clubs: Ajax in Holland (2002-07), Real Madrid in Spain (2007-09), Inter Milan in Italy (2009-13), Galatasary (2013-present)

Position: Midfield

First break: At seven years old, Sneijder joined Ajax's youth academy in Amsterdam. Like Barcelona's 'La Masia', the Ajax academy is famous for producing some of the best players in Europe. He made his first team debut for Ajax at 18.

Major achievements: He has won the Dutch league with Ajax (2003-04) and the Spanish league with Real Madrid (2007-08). In the 2009-10 season he won the 'treble' with Inter Milan – the Italian league, Italian Cup and the UEFA Champions League.

Secrets of success: At 5ft 7in, Sneijder is relatively short, but he is fast and strong on the ball. Like David Beckham he is a 'dead ball specialist' – he has been the first-choice free kick taker for all the teams he has played for.

To help him practise with his weaker left foot, Ajax coaches blew a whistle and stopped training every time Sneijder touched the ball with his right foot!

Life Story

The 2009-10 season put Wesley Sneijder on the map. The Dutch-born attacking midfielder won the domestic treble with Inter Milan, and then helped Holland to their third World Cup Final. Sneijder was the tournament's joint top scorer with five goals.

He spent the early part of his career with Ajax before a move to Real Madrid in Spain. The transfer fee of €27 million (£22 million) made him the second most expensive Dutch player ever, behind Ruud van Nistelrooy.

Questions and Answers

Q Which position do you most enjoy playing in?

A "I think I play best right behind the strikers, as an attacking midfielder. I like the coach to give me freedom, thanks to which I score many goals."

Wesley Sneijder, realmadridportal.com, August 2008

Q What made you leave Holland and start playing abroad?

A "It's hard to explain... There comes a time in which a football player suddenly wants more. I'd played in the Dutch League for five years and I had a very good run... which gave me the chance of joining Real Madrid. You have to grab that chance and do things well in order to be able to say you made the right decision."

Wesley Sneijder, bbc.co.uk, 2008

Sneijder dribbles the ball past Russia's Zyryanov in Euro 2008.

He got off to a great start with a goal on his debut for the Spanish side, but unfortunately suffered a serious knee injury in his second season and struggled to regain his place in the team.

When Madrid sold Sneijder to Inter Milan for around half of what they had paid for him, everyone assumed his best performances were behind him. However, a glittering first season at Inter Milan, and an eye-catching World Cup, have made Sneijder an international talent to watch.

David Beckham

GREAT BRITON

Beckham was the England player liaison at the World Cup in 2010.

Beckham says if he didn't play football, he would like to build Lego for a living!

Stats!

Name: David Robert Joseph Beckham

Date of birth: 2 May 1975

Clubs: Manchester United (1993-2003), Real Madrid in Spain (2003-2007), Los Angeles Galaxy (2007-2012), AC Milan on loan (2009 and 2010), Paris St-Germain (2013-present)

Position: Midfielder

First break: Beckham had youth trials with Tottenham Hotspur, Leyton Orient and Norwich City, but signed for Manchester United on his 14th birthday. Alongside players such as Ryan Giggs and Paul Scholes, he won the FA Youth Cup in 1992 and made his first team debut in the same year.

Major achievements: With Manchester United he won the Premier League six times (1995-96, 1996-97, 1998-99, 1999-2000, 2000-01, 2002-03), the FA Cup twice (1996, 1999) and the UEFA Champions League (1999). He also won the Spanish League with Real Madrid (2006-07). He was England Captain from 2000-2006.

Secrets of success: At his peak, Beckham was recognised as the best crosser of the ball, and the best free kick taker in the world. Manchester United manager Alex Ferguson said, he 'practised with a discipline to achieve an accuracy that other players wouldn't care about'.

Life Story

David Beckham is one of the most talented, and certainly the most famous, footballer that Britain has ever produced. The Londoner left home at 14 to join his boyhood idols, Manchester United. He rose through the ranks alongside a talented generation of young players, and in ten years with the first team he won every prize in the English game, including the Premier League, FA Cup and Champions League.

In 2003, Beckham moved to Real Madrid in Spain for £28 million. He quickly became a favourite with the fans at the club because of his skills and hard work. In his final season in Spain, he helped Madrid win the Spanish league title.

When playing for Los Angeles Galaxy in the United States, Beckham's worldwide popularity helped to raise the profile of football – or 'soccer' as it's known there – in a country where the sport has to compete with basketball, baseball and American football for the fans' attention.

Beckham with LA Galaxy in 2009.

Questions and Answers

Q What have you learned from the managers you've worked with?

A "I've been lucky to work with some of the greatest managers in football. Sir Alex Ferguson was like a father to me... He looked after me all the way up to the time I left [the club]... Fabio Capello is different tactically, he's Italian, they're best at that."

Q How did you get so good at free kicks?

A "I go through situations the night before, sometimes I even lie awake at night thinking about [what to do]... When kids ask me what they have to do to become a professional, I tell them to practise. I'm 35 and I still practise!"

David Beckham, the *Mirror*, July 2010 (both quotes)

Beckham married former Spice Girls singer Victoria Adams in 1999. The couple, who have four children, Brooklyn, Romeo, Cruz and Harper, are never far from newspaper headlines.

Andrés Iniesta

PASS MASTER

Iniesta and the Spanish team received a heroes' welcome in Barcelona after winning the World Cup in 2010.

Stats!

Name: Andrés Iniesta Luján

Date of birth: 11 May 1984

Clubs: Barcelona (2002-present)

Position: Midfield

First break: Iniesta was spotted by Barcelona scouts as a 12 year old playing for his local youth team. The club invited him to become part of their famous 'La Masia' training academy, where fellow players Lionel Messi and Cesc Fabregas were also students. Iniesta had to leave home and move 500km (300 miles) across the country to join.

Major achievements: He has won the Spanish league four times with Barcelona (2004-05, 2005-06, 2008-09, 2009-10), the Champions League three times (2006, 2009, 2012) and was named UEFA Best Player in Europe in 2012. He won Euro 2008 and the 2010 World Cup with Spain.

Secrets of success: From as young as eight, Iniesta was determined to succeed. Twice a week he left school at lunchtime, travelled 45 minutes each way to practise with his youth side, and then came back to his school desk for his afternoon lessons. He was exhausted, but happy!

Iniesta's grandfather ran the village pub. The whole family worked there, except young Andrés. He was always too busy playing football!

Life Story

After Barcelona beat Manchester United 2-0 in the 2009 Champions League final, Wayne Rooney described Andrés Iniesta as the best player in the world. Playing in a Barcelona team alongside World Footballer of the Year Lionel Messi, that was quite an achievement!

Iniesta plays as an attacking midfielder for Barcelona and for his country. He and fellow midfielder Xavi Hernández share an unspoken understanding of each other's games, and together have conquered Europe and the world.

Questions and Answers

Q **What was it like moving so far away from your family at 12?**

A "The first few months were hell. I only saw my parents once or twice a month... I was lucky to have fantastic mates like [Carlos] Puyol and Victor Valdes... They helped me get used to my situation."

Andrés Iniesta, bbc.co.uk, 2010

Q **Why do you think Spain are currently so successful?**

A "[Fellow midfielder] Xavi and I have played together for years... and sometimes you don't need to think or look to know where he will be or what he's going to do. But we have also benefitted from Cesc [Fabregas]... [David] Villa... and so on – the style of all the players fits together so well."

Andrés Iniesta, fourfourtwo.com, June 2010

In fact, in a moment straight out of a school boy's wildest fantasy, it was Iniesta who scored the goal in extra time that helped Spain win the 2010 World Cup.

The midfielder is willing and able to play anywhere on the pitch to help his team – from winger to central midfield to second striker. His abilities have prompted Barcelona to add a £120 million buyout clause to his contract to scare off any clubs who might want to buy him!

Iniesta prepares to score the winning goal in the World Cup Final against the Netherlands in 2010.

19

Rio Ferdinand

WORLD-CLASS DEFENDER

The England captain Rio Ferdinand in May 2010.

Apart from playing football, Rio Ferdinand has launched an Internet magazine (www.rioferdinand.com) and produced a Hollywood movie!

Stats!

Name: Rio Gavin Ferdinand

Date of birth: 7 November 1978

Clubs: West Ham United (1995-2000), Leeds United (2000-02), Manchester United (2002-present)

Position: Central defender

First break: Ferdinand joined West Ham's youth academy in 1992 after being spotted by Frank Lampard's father. Lampard was also a trainee at the academy.

Major achievements: He has won the Premier League with Manchester United four times - 2002-03, 2006-07, 2007-08 and 2008-09. They also won the Champions League in 2008, beating Chelsea in the final.

Secrets of success: Ferdinand grew up on a poor housing estate in south-east London. However, the guidance and advice of his parents kept him away from gangs and violence. At 11 years old, he won a scholarship to the Central School of Ballet in London, travelling to classes four days a week for four years. The ballet training improved his balance and strength. Ferdinand was nicknamed 'Pele' by his first youth coach for his composure on the ball.

Life Story

Rio Ferdinand is one of England's most talented defenders. A strong header of the ball, with excellent positional sense and a will-to-win attitude, he is often compared to Bobby Moore, England's 1966 World Cup winning captain. Ferdinand has played a big part in Manchester United's success.

The defender spent five years with West Ham United, alongside fellow England stars Frank Lampard and Joe Cole. When he joined Leeds United for £18 million in 2000 he became Britain's most expensive defender. Then he joined Manchester United in 2002 for £29.1 million and became the most expensive British footballer in history!

Ferdinand with Manchester United plays in the FA Premier League in 2010.

Questions and Answers

Q Why do you think you succeeded as a footballer?

A "I always wanted to be a professional footballer, and there was nothing really going to get in my way. I used to leave my mates on the estate and take trains and buses to West Ham. That was my whole life when I was growing up."

Q What skills does it take to be a good captain?

A "There are different types of leaders. There's the guy who shouts and screams, and the guy who leads by example. I do a bit of both. I lead by example, but when somebody needs to be told I never shirk that responsibility."

Rio Ferdinand, the *Guardian*, March 2010 (both quotes)

Ferdinand has played over 80 times for England, making his debut in 1997 at 19 years old. He played well for his country in the 2002 and 2006 World Cups, but unfortunately a knee ligament injury kept him out of the 2010 World Cup in South Africa. In typical fashion, he was fighting for his place again as soon as he was fit. He hoped to captain his country at the 2012 European Championships, but was left out of the squad.

Lionel Messi

Career

Background: Messi and his family left Argentina for Spain when he was just 13. Football talent scouts had seen him playing for local team Newell's Old Boys and recommended him to Barcelona. The club paid for expensive growth hormone treatment to help the player reach his current height of 5ft 7in.

Current club: FC Barcelona (Spain) 2003-present.

International team: Argentina 2005-present.

Career highs: Won six trophies with Barcelona during the 2008-09 season, including the Spanish League and the Champions League. Was named FIFA World Player of the Year in 2009. Scored 45 goals (including 34 in the league) for Barcelona in 2009-10 season.

Special skills: One of the best dribblers in the world. Excellent ball control, powerful left-foot shot.

Website: www.lionelmessi.com

Basic Information

Home: Born in Rosario, Argentina. Lives in Barcelona, Spain.

Birthday: 24 June 1987

Ryan Giggs

Career

Background: Was signed by Manchester United manager Alex Ferguson at 14 when he watched Giggs score a hat trick against a Man Utd Under-15 side. Made his professional debut in 1991 and has been in the team ever since. Holds the record for most Manchester United appearances.

Current club: Manchester United 1990-present.

International team: Wales 1991-2007.

Career highs: Giggs has won more medals than any other player in English football history. Currently holds 11 league title medals, two Champions League medals and four FA Cup medals. Was voted PFA Player of the Year, and BBC Sports Personality of the Year in 2009.

Special skills: Great speed in his youth. With age, he has moved into centre midfield to maximise his great passing abilities.

Website: www.ryangiggs.cc

Basic Information

Home: Born in Cardiff, Wales. Lives in Manchester, England.

Birthday: 29 November 1973

Thomas Müller

Career

Background: Müller joined Bayern Munich at ten years old and worked his way up through youth and reserve teams, making his professional debut in 2008. Signed his first senior contract in February 2009, and broke into the first team, and the German national team, during the 2009-10 season.

Current club: Bayern Munich (Germany) 2008-present.

International team: Germany 2010-present.

Career highs: Won the German league and cup double with Bayern in 2010. Reached the semi-finals of the 2010 World Cup, before losing 1-0 to Spain. Müller was named best Young Player at the tournament, and won the Golden Boot for top scorer.

Special skills: Müller is adaptable, and can play as a winger, attacking midfielder or striker. Quick and a regular goal scorer.

Website: http:// en.wikipedia.org/wiki/Thomas_Müller_(footballer)

Basic Information

Home: Born in Weilheim, West Germany. Lives in Munich, Germany.

Birthday: 13 September 1989

Cesc Fàbregas

Career

Background: Fàbregas started as a trainee with his local club Barcelona, but joined Arsenal as a 16 year old, becoming the Gunners' youngest ever player. Established himself as a first team regular in the 2004-05 season, and was made the club's captain in 2008.

Current club: Barcelona 2011-present.

International team: Spain 2006-present.

Career highs: Won the 2005 FA Cup and the 2007 League Cup with Arsenal. He was voted PFA Young Player of the Year in 2008. Has won both the 2008 European Championship, and the 2010 World Cup with Spain.

Special skills: Fàbregas is a 'playmaker' – he makes things happen for the team with his passing abilities, and his eye for space and opportunities. He also takes most of Arsenal's free kicks, corners and penalties.

Website: www.cescfabregas.com/en

Basic Information

Home: Born in Vilassar de Mar, Spain. Lives in London, England.
Birthday: 4 May 1987

Diego Forlán

Career

Background: Forlán was born into a family of footballers. His father played for Uruguay in the 1966 and 1974 World Cups, and his grandfather played for Independiente in Argentina. Young Forlán also had four successful years at Independiente, before joining Manchester Utd, and then on to Villarreal and Atlético Madrid in Spain, and Inter-Milan in Italy.

Current club: Internacional 2012-present.

International team: Uruguay 2002-present.

Career highs: Won the Premier League with Manchester Utd in 2002-03, and the UEFA Europa League with Atlético Madrid in 2009-10. Was presented with the Golden Ball as the best player of the 2010 World Cup.

Special skills: Forlán is a prolific goal scorer who is strong in the air and comfortable shooting with either foot.

Website: www.diegoforlan.com/

Basic Information

Home: Born in Montevideo, Uruguay. Lives in Madrid, Spain.
Birthday: 19 May 1979

Didier Drogba

Career

Background: Drogba made his debut at 18 for French second division club Le Mans. He didn't sign a professional contract until he was 21. Drogba played for Guincamp and Olympique de Marseille in the French first division before moving to Chelsea between 2004-2012. He joined Shangai Shenhua in 2012, but left in early 2013 due to an ongoing contract dispute.

Current club: Galatasaray 2013-present.

International team: Ivory Coast 2002-present.

Career highs: Has won the Premier League three times (2004-05, 2005-06 and 2009-10) and the FA Cup three times (2007, 2009, 2010) with Chelsea. Was the Premier League's top scorer in 2007 and 2010. Voted African Footballer of the Year in 2006 and 2009. He scored the winning penalty in the 2012 Champions League final.

Special skills: Drogba is very strong, with a powerful and accurate shot. He is a great 'finisher' – when he gets a chance to score, he rarely misses!

Website: www.didierdrogba.com/en/

Basic Information

Home: Born in Abidjan, Ivory Coast. Lives in London, England.
Birthday: 11 March 1978

More stars to look out for

Theo Walcott
Xavi Hernández
Fernando Torres
Jack Wilshere
Arjen Robben

Marouane Chamakh
Joe Hart
Yaya Toure
Michael Essien
Javier Hernández

Index